EASTERN HEMIS

MW01132062

EUROPE

ASIA

AFRICA

PACIFIC
OCEAN

ATLANTIC
OCEAN

INDIAN
OCEAN

AUSTRALIA

To
my mother
Joan.
100% Saint Lucian!

Marco's Travels – Sa ka fèt, Saint Lucia!

Text copyright 2017 © By Jason Louis.

Illustrations copyright 2017 © Jason Louis

Illustrated and designed by AFI Digital Services LLP

Manufactured in the US

Summary: Marco embarks on another of his adventures, traveling to Saint Lucia to visit his friend Trevor, who takes him on a journey around the island where he experiences the Saint Lucian culture, attractions and hospitality.

International Standard Book Number

ISBN -13-978-0-9903267-7-9

www.marcostravels.com

Sa ka fèt, Saint Lucia!

It was a busy summer for Marco, visiting friends, spending time with Grandma, and finally getting a fish tank. Before heading back to school, he had one more trip planned: a visit to Saint Lucia to see his friend Trevor.

"Marco, you'll love the warm weather, the friendly people, the beaches, and ohhh, the food," teased Trevor.

Marco could hardly contain himself. "I'll see you soon," he said, grinning with excitement.

Marco spun his globe. Saint Lucia is a Caribbean island located in the northern hemisphere, on the North American continent.

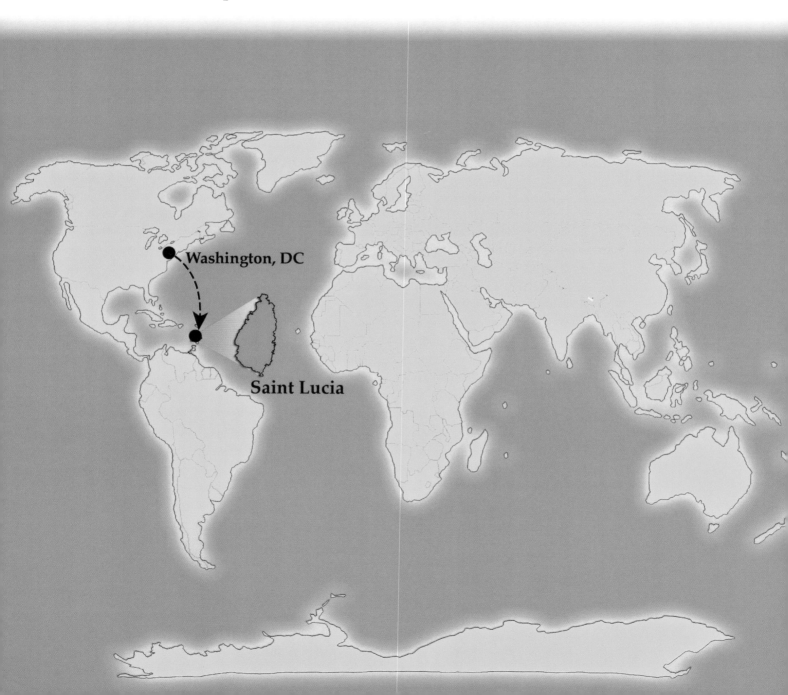

The island has a population of 179,000 people. To get there, Marco had to travel south over the Atlantic Ocean before landing in Castries, the capital.

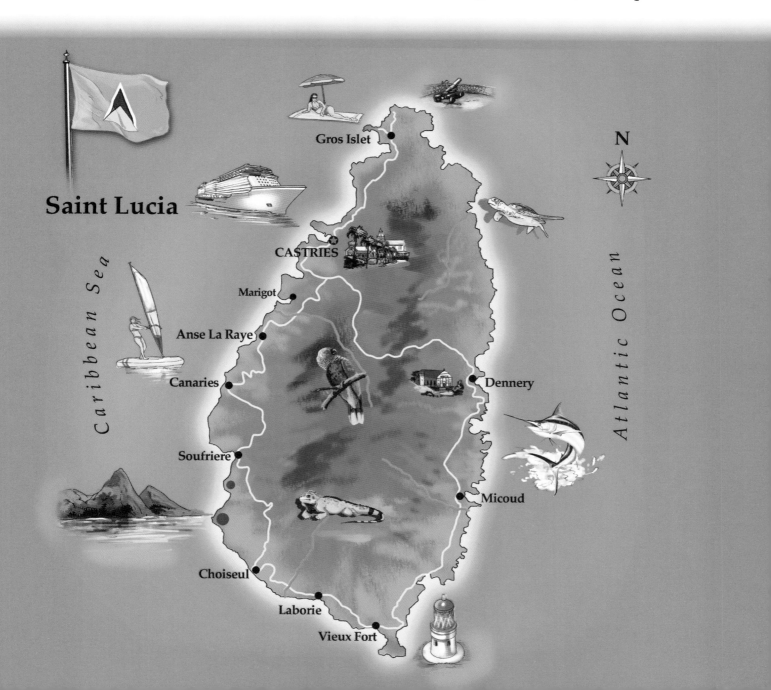

Saint Lucia

N

Caribbean Sea

Atlantic Ocean

Gros Islet

CASTRIES

Marigot

Anse La Raye

Canaries

Dennery

Soufriere

Micoud

Choiseul

Laborie

Vieux Fort

Marco arrived on the island to the sound of calypso, a popular type of Caribbean music with West African and French influence.

"Marco, *sa ka fèt?*" greeted Trevor, which means "How are you?" or "What's happening?" in *Kwéyòl*, a French-based creole language spoken on the island in addition to English, the official language.

"Welcome to Saint Lucia!" added Linda, Trevor's mom.
"Thanks for inviting me. I'm excited to be here!" replied Marco.

Marco arrived at Trevor's house. It was situated on a hill with a view of the Caribbean Sea. Trevor's dad John and his sister Beverley welcomed him. As Marco made his way through the house, he noticed crowns and sashes on the table.

"What are these for?" he asked.

"These are for an upcoming festival," replied Trevor. "It's going to be fun."

"Tomorrow, we'll take a trip around the island. We'll also stop by Uncle Son Son's," said John.

"Can we go around the entire island in a day?" asked Marco.

"Yes!" replied Trevor. "You'll love it."

The next day, John and Trevor took Marco on a trip around the island. The first stop was at the Castries Market, where they picked up a few local craft items. They then drove along the west coast, stopping at Marigot Bay before reaching the town of Soufriere.

In the background, Marco noticed two mountains rising from the sea.
"Those are called the Pitons and are a World Heritage site," said Trevor. "The smaller one, *Petit Piton*, is closer, and the bigger one, *Gros Piton* is farther back."
"I would love a picture with the Pitons in the background," said Marco.

They drove through Soufriere toward another popular attraction, the Sulphur Springs.

"What that smell?" asked Marco. "It's like rotten eggs."

"That's sulphur, and it comes from the Sulphur Springs. It's an inactive volcano that you can drive right into," replied Trevor.

"What? Drive into a volcano?" asked Marco.

"Don't worry, you'll be safe," Trevor assured him.

They walked into the volcano. Hot water bubbled and steam rose from the crater. "This is unbelievable!" said Marco.

"You can even take a bath in the dark, warm water downstream," suggested Trevor.

"No thanks, I'll pass," responded Marco.

They continued their trip around the island, stopping at Uncle Son Son's house in the village of Micoud on the east coast.

"Marco, *sa ka fèt?*" greeted Uncle Son Son. "Welcome to Micoud."

"Thanks," replied Marco, noticing kids playing in the yard.

Trevor explained. "These girls are playing a game called *tiki-tok*. You win by collecting the most pebbles.

This boy is having fun pushing an old tire around with sticks, and my cousin Mark is playing with his handmade toy truck, built using stuff you would usually throw away."

"That truck looks amazing! Can I take a turn?" asked Marco.

"Sure," replied Mark, handing over the control stick to Marco.

"This is so much fun!" hollered Marco as he drove the truck around the yard.

"It's time to go, boys," said John.
"Thanks for stopping by," said Uncle Son Son, handing John a fruit basket to take home.

On the way home, Marco noticed many places with French names.
"Saint Lucia was once a French colony," informed John. "Centuries ago, the French and British fought over Saint Lucia fourteen times. Although the British won, the French influence is still everywhere."

"Tomorrow, we'll head to Pigeon Island for a beach picnic with Aunty Joan. She cooks the most delicious food," said John.

The next day, the entire family headed to Pigeon Island, a national landmark located on the northern tip of the island. It has two beaches, a fort, and the ruins of military buildings used during wars between the British and French.

When they arrived, Aunty Joan was already there. "You boys should visit the fort while I get the food ready," she suggested.

The boys immediately headed to the fort, making their way onto the platform at the highest point.

"What's that?" asked Marco, pointing to a large rusty object on the platform. "That's a cannon," replied Trevor. "The British and French used cannons to fight each other, but don't worry, this one is very old and doesn't work anymore."

Relieved, Marco looked toward the northwest coastline, admiring the panoramic view. "Wow, it's beautiful from up here."

"Let's go back. Lunch should be ready now," said Trevor. The boys headed down to the beach.

Trevor described the food on the picnic table. "This is cooked green bananas, which we call *green figs*. Over here is salted cod, locally called *saltfish*. *Green figs* and *saltfish* is Saint Lucia's national dish. On the left is *breadfruit*, next to it, some *dasheen*. In the red dish, stewed chicken. And here is some salad. We also have hot pepper sauce to add more flavor, but you can skip that."

Marco's mouth started watering.

"Over here we have lime juice mixed with banana essence called *squash*, and in this pitcher, *soursop* juice. For dessert we have mangoes and these local sweets. The brown cubes are called *guava cheese*, in this container *tamarind balls*, and these brown clusters are *coconut tablets*."

The food was so delicious Marco had seconds.

After lunch, the boys spent the rest of the time on the beach, bathing in the warm, blue Caribbean Sea.

The next day, the boys were up early.

"What's this festival we're taking part in?" asked Marco.

"It's a flower festival called *la woz*, which means rose," answered Trevor. "Let's get dressed."

La woz is one of two flower festivals celebrated on the island; the other is *la magwit* or marguerite. Each group has a formal structure with a king, queen, princes, princesses, and other symbolic roles such as judges, nurses, soldiers, and policemen.

Each group also has a singer, called a *chantwèl*, who leads all night singing and dancing sessions called *séances*. On their feast day, members dress up in various outfits representing their respective roles and parade through the streets ahead of their grand celebration.

Marco joined the parade dressed as a policeman, while Trevor dressed as a prince. They paraded through the streets singing and dancing all the way to a hall to celebrate and feast.

"It's time to go, boys," John summoned. "Marco is leaving tomorrow."

Marco was having so much fun, he was sad the festival had come to an end.

"I've had such a great time, I can't believe I have to leave," said Marco.
Trevor handed him a locally made toy truck as a token of their friendship.
"Wow! Thank you," exclaimed Marco.

Marco boarded the plane, remembering the warm weather and friendly people.

As he waved goodbye, he started thinking about his next trip. He had no idea where he would visit, but he knew he wanted it to be just as exciting.

Saint Lucia

Basic Facts and Glossary of Terms

Basic Facts: Saint Lucia

Population: 179,000*

Capital City: Castries

Official Languages: English

Other Language Spoken: Kwéyòl

Location (Continent): North America

Area: 238 Sq. Mi. (617 Sq. Kilometers)

Currency: East Caribbean Dollar

National Dish: Green Fig and Saltfish

National Bird: Jacquot (Amazona Versicolor)

National Dress: Wob Dwiyet (for women)

Popular Tourist Attractions: Pitons (World Heritage Site), Sulphur Springs

Popular Sports: Cricket, Football (Soccer)

Popular Music: Calypso, Soca, Zouk, Country, Reggae

Popular Cultural Festivals: La Woz (Rose), La Magwit (Marguerite), Jounen Kwéyòl

*Population statistics by UN World Population Prospects; 2017 Revision

Kwéyòl - Common Terms

What's up or What's going on?: Sa ka fèt?

Good Morning/Good Day: Bon jou

How are you?: Kouman ou yé

Good bye: Babay!, Dédé

Good Night: Bonswè

Yes: Wi

No: Non

Please: Souplé

Friend: Jan

Thanks: Mèci

Me: Mwen

You: Ou

Come Here: Vini

Good afternoon: Bonn apwémidi

I Don't Know: Ma sav

How much is this?: Konmen pou sa?

Food: Manjé

Drink: Bwè

Let's go: An alé, Annou alé

Today: Jòdi, Jòdi-a

Tomorrow: Denmen

Yesterday: Yè

From the Author
"Saint Lucia"

Nicknamed the "Helen of the West Indies" for its astonishing beauty, it's very easy to see why the British and the French went to war repeatedly for this island. Lush rain forest, majestic mountains and spectacular scenery, all add to make the island truly beautiful.

Add the friendly people, great food and the *Kwéyòl* language, and it's a cultural experience that's truly unique. There is so much to see and do on the island. You can choose to bargain at the century old Castries Market, spend some time at one of the many white sand beaches or stop in the town of Gros Islet, for the popular Friday night street party.

The "round-the-island" trip is a must. Take some time to stop at the small, quaint, sea-side towns and villages, and inland communities, to experience the true *"Lucian"* culture and hospitality. You may even be tempted to play *tiki-tok* or roll a *sec*. Don't forget to try a mango (eat using your hands), local bread and the jelly of a coconut.

If along the way someone asks, *"sa ka fèt?"*. Keep calm and show that you're well versed in the *Kwéyòl* language by responding, *"mwen la"*.

Saint Lucia is truly special and I am happy that I still call this island, home.

EASTERN HEMISPHERE

EUROPE

ASIA

AFRICA

PACIFIC
OCEAN

ATLANTIC
OCEAN

INDIAN
OCEAN

AUSTRALIA

93372389R00024

Made in the USA
Columbia, SC
13 April 2018